THE KINDLE WRITING BIBLE

HOW TO WRITE A BESTSELLING NONFICTION BOOK FROM START TO FINISH

TOM CORSON-KNOWLES

Get the free Kindle publishing and marketing video training series here:

www.EbookPublishingSchool.com

Earnings Disclaimer

When addressing financial matters in any of books, sites, videos, newsletters or other content, we've taken every effort to ensure we accurately represent our products and services and their ability to improve your life or grow your business. However, there is no guarantee that you will get any results or earn any money using any of our ideas, tools, strategies or recommendations, and we do not purport any "get rich schemes" in any of our content. Nothing in this book is a promise or guarantee of earnings. Your level of success in attaining similar results is dependent upon a number of factors including your skill, knowledge, ability, dedication, business savvy, network, and financial situation, to name a few. Because these factors differ according to individuals, we cannot and do not guarantee your success, income level, or ability to earn revenue. You alone are responsible for your actions and results in life and business. Any forward-looking statements outlined in this book or on our Sites are simply our opinion and thus are not guarantees or promises for actual performance. It should be clear to you that by law we make no guarantees that you will achieve any results from our ideas or models presented in this book or on our Sites, and we offer no professional legal, medical, psychological or financial advice.

Why I Wrote This Book

I've got a secret that you would NEVER know... but I'm going to tell it to you right now. I don't want to write this book.

That's right – as I'm sitting at my desk right now overlooking the gorgeous mountains in Hawaii, I simply don't want to write this book. I'd rather be outside hiking the world-renowned Na Pali coastline, surfing 20 foot waves or soaking up the sun on a secluded island beach. But I'm not doing any of those things right now – I'm writing.

And that's the "secret to success" as they say. How do you sit down and make yourself write, even when you don't want to? Even when you don't feel like it? What do you do if you're bored, uncomfortable or even afraid of failure or rejection? What do you do if you don't even know HOW to write a book, let alone turn it into a bestseller?

Who writes books these days anyway?

Well, this book you're reading right now is a labor of love, that's for darn sure! But the truth is, all of my writing is a labor of love (with only a very few exceptions). If you don't love writing, sharing, teaching and inspiring others, then don't do it. Don't waste your time doing something that you don't love to do and that doesn't inspire you.

If you do love writing, though, this book is for you. If you've dreamed of writing a book but never figured out how, this book is for you. If you have an important message inside you that you want to share with the world, this book is for you. If you want to write a book but aren't a good writer or don't enjoy writing and want to find alternative ways to get your message out there, then you will love this book!

For me, writing itself is not the most enjoyable thing in the world. I honestly would rather be hiking right now to a secret waterfall hidden in the cliffs that has scarcely been seen by another human.

But even though I don't always like writing, I do love to write! I know you're thinking, "hey, hold on Tom – you just said you don't like to write but now you're saying you love to write. What's the deal?"

The deal is this – there's a difference between loving something and liking something. For example, I like to eat crème brulee. It's delicious! But I don't love eating crème brulee. I don't stay awake at night, thinking about it. I don't dream of the perfect crème brulee. In fact, I haven't even had crème brulee in probably over a year, even though I really do like it a lot. Eating crème brulee is a pleasure – it's a treat, and I thoroughly enjoy it when I do eat it.

On the other hand, I love writing. I think about it day and night. I've been writing poetry since I was a teenager and books since I was 19. When I first started writing poetry and books, I never even expected my work to be published or read by many people. It was really just for me! I guess you could say I'm a selfish writer because most of the time when I write, I'm writing for myself and not for you, the reader.

That doesn't mean I don't care about you – I do! I love my readers just like I love my writing. But when I'm in the creative act of writing itself, I'm not even thinking about you, the reader. In fact, I'm not even thinking about anything – I'm just writing. I'm "in the flow" as Mihaly Csikszentmihalyi talks about in his groundbreaking book, *Flow.*

Sometimes I'll get so engrossed in my writing, I'll look up at the clock and two, four, even six hours have gone by and I didn't even realize it! Sometimes I'll look up at the clock—it's 1am in the morning, and I can't even remember having dinner! That's how much I love writing. That's how I get into the flow.

And I've got some advice for you—if you want to succeed as a writer long-term, you better get into the flow. You better fall in love with your writing or you won't keep it up. Sure, anyone can write one or two books. But what are you going to do after that?

If you want to be a truly successful author, I mean in the top 1% of 1% of all authors, you have to love what you do. There's just no other way around it.

That's the bad news.

The good news is that you can learn to fall in love with writing. I wrote this book to teach you how to fall in love with writing and become a successful nonfiction author.

Oh, and even if you write fiction you'll still love this book.

TABLE OF CONTENTS

THE PHILOSOPHY OF WRITING NONFICTION

My philosophy for writing nonfiction is this: I write to provide solutions for my readers' problems.

I'm guessing you have a problem: you either want to learn how to write a book or how to write a book better. In either case, I've got the solution to your problem.

If you want to write a memoir or autobiography, that's all fine and dandy but it's not what I do personally. Almost all of the strategies in this book will apply to you if that's what you're writing about, or even if you write fiction. But when I write books, I focus on solving problems for people. After all, who would buy a book called "How To Write Better" if they didn't want to write?

Make sure that your nonfiction book is solving a problem or else ask yourself, "What's the point?" Sometimes the point is you just want to write for yourself. Sometimes you want to document your life story or history. Sometimes you just want to have fun and create something new on paper. All of that is just fine and wonderful. But if you want to be really, really successful as a nonfiction author, in my experience, you have to solve a problem for your reader.

Ask yourself, "What problem do I want to solve for people?" Is it just entertainment you want to provide? Do you have some specific strategies and ideas that can help people live happier, healthier or more fun lives? Do you know some unique way of creating art or the fundamental techniques to success in a sport? Whatever your expertise is, use it to create a book that not only helps people solve a problem but helps earn you a great income from royalties as well.

CHAPTER 1
OLD VS. NEW

The tools available to writers like you and me today have revolutionized the writing and publishing industry.

Can you imagine that just a few thousand years ago people used to write books by using pointed rocks to make carvings in even bigger rocks? Imagine how long it would have taken to write a novel or a how-to book back then! Just a few hundred years ago, the most basic printing presses were created and they revolutionized the writing industry. Then computers came around and changed the industry again. Today, anyone with $200 can get a netbook and write using a word processor. The game has changed!

And it's changed so much and so fast, few people really appreciate this dramatic change. It's so EASY now to write a book. Anyone can do it!

Not only is writing easy now but publishing is easy too! Anyone can self-publish a book on Amazon Kindle for free. All it takes is a few dollars for a cover design, everything else you can learn to do yourself. And for those who can't afford a $5 cover design from Fiverr.com, you can create your own cover design using free graphics software!

Funny story – when my brother found out I was doing so well with Kindle publishing he said, "Hey I've been thinking about publishing my senior thesis on Burma. Do you think I could do that?" I said, "Duh! Of course you can." So I showed him how to upload his senior thesis and without even having a book cover or doing any marketing, he started selling about 1 copy a day at $3.95. Now that's not life-changing money – but imagine if he had published his thesis when he first wrote it – almost 10 years ago!

The point is – he missed out on a lot of money because he didn't understand the digital publishing revolution. Likewise, I missed out on a lot of money by not understanding how to self-publish sooner. I'm guessing you're probably thinking now, "I've missed out on a lot of money too!" That's okay – let's not worry about the past. Let's just move forward and start making some more money while helping our readers solve their problems. Sound good?

So now you understand just how easy it is today to write and publish a book. Sure, you have to learn HOW to do it (which is where *The Kindle Writing Bible* series comes in). But it's essentially a very simple process.

Like I said, anyone can write and publish a book these days (trust me, if my brother can do it, you can too).

The problems you and I have as writers are the eternal problems of the human condition. "What's easy to do is just as easy not to do" as my mentor Jim Rohn said often.

All of the seemingly insurmountable obstacles we face today are internal obstacles, not external. What holds us back is our fear, procrastination, indecision, lack of vision, lack of knowledge and insecurity (and you'll learn how to conquer these obstacles later on in this book). You have to realize now that it is NOT writing a book that holds you back. It's not the publishing industry holding you back. The only excuse you have for not succeeding as an author today is yourself! That's the good news. The game has changed. The only question is, are you ready to play the game? And how well will you play it?

I want you to really appreciate where you are right now. Sitting there, reading this on your Kindle or smartphone or computer... you have to realize you have it so easy when it comes to writing and publishing books these days! I'm constantly grateful for this incredible opportunity we have as writers today. It has truly changed my life. I hope it will change your life as well.

As Jim Rohn says, *"the key is to work harder on yourself than you do on your job."* This book is all about how to do your job – how to become a great writer. But it's also about how you can work on yourself to become a better person and overcome those internal obstacles that keep most writers broke and embarrassed.

Always remember... *"the key is to work harder on yourself than you do on your job."* When you become a better, stronger, more confident person, you will see your success as a writer grow in ways you could never have imagined before. I'm wishing you the best of success!

CHAPTER 2
THE ANATOMY OF A NONFICTION BOOK

So many people have asked me what a nonfiction book should look like, how many pages it should be and what it should include so I want to make sure you understand the anatomy of a nonfiction book – both for eBooks and print books.

Pages and Word Counts

How long should a good book be?

Most publishers say 250 words equals one book page, while some writers say 400. The answer lies somewhere in between most likely. But page count isn't really what's important for me – word count is much more important, in my opinion, because it's the words of your book that determine how long it will take to read.

For example, if you have a 100 page book and 60 of those pages are just pictures, readers will read it just about as fast as they would a 40 page book with no pictures.

However, it's very hard for readers or publishers even to think about word count – so when you're describing or selling your book to the public or a publisher, always give them page length numbers. It's much easier to visualize "a 93-page Facebook marketing action guide" than a "21,327 word long book on Facebook marketing."

For nonfiction Kindle books or eBooks, anywhere from 10,000 words and up is just fine. I've seen eBooks that were less than 10,000 words and they're just too short, even for the most niche or tiny subjects. Give your readers some valuable substance and make sure your eBooks are not much less than 10,000 words.

Some Kindle Singles titles are 5,000 to 8,000 words long and that's nice for a short story but it can be quite brief for a helpful nonfiction book.

So how long should a book be? There is no one answer! The best answer I've found is that a nonfiction book should be long enough to give the reader what they want. If that's 8,000 words or 83,000 doesn't really matter to me, although it certainly takes longer to write 83,000 words.

I try to keep my books short and to the point because I value my time and I value my reader's time. I read about 300 books a year, if not more, and I read almost exclusively nonfiction. It's disgusting to me how much of these books are filled with fluff that provides NO VALUE to the reader.

I really don't care about all the publishing agents and your graphic designer that you spend 4 pages thanking in your Acknowledgements section of your book. I don't care about your dog Fluffy or you wife's family. I just want the facts! Give me the information, the meat, the substance. Don't bore me with all that other stuff.

Well, that's just my personal opinion so that's how I write – short and to the point. I don't want to waste my reader's time and I like to think they appreciate that.

Action Steps

Action steps should be included in all of your nonfiction books if they are to be instructive to the reader. You'll notice many action steps in this book. You must tell your reader what to do and encourage them to do it now!

It's well-known in the personal development and online marketing communities that only a very small percentage of customers ever actually implement the information in the courses, books, seminars and workshops they invest in. I don't know about you, but I write books to help people change their lives. So if you want to do that, you'd better tell your readers to take action steps and to do them now!

Organization

The truth is, most of the information out there that people buy books to learn is available for free online. Despite the fact that millions of weight loss books are sold every year, there are millions if not billions of articles online about how to lose weight! And it's all available for free. So why would anyone ever buy a weight loss book with all that free information?

There are several reasons but one of the biggest reasons in my opinion is for organization, guidance and action steps. People don't want to spend 8 hours online trying to find information on weight loss. They want it simple and easy. That's why they might buy your weight loss book!

People buy your nonfiction books to save themselves time, money, energy and effort. Therefore, you should focus on saving your readers money, time, energy and effort! If you can do that, you'll be delivering great value to your readers and they will love you.

CHAPTER 3
CHOOSING YOUR TOPIC

The first step in writing a book is to decide on your topic. The key is to focus on one book and complete it and then move on to others. That's easier said than done!

I often find myself coming up with dozens of exciting book ideas in a very short period of time. I'm usually writing 2 or 3 or more books at a time. But the key, I've found, is to focus on just **completing one book at a time**.

It's hard to start a new project. Many people procrastinate and put off starting something new. So starting is a huge key to success. But finishing is just as important! You can start 1,000 books but if you never finish, what's the point? Always finish what you start! Even if it sucks. Just finish it.

Cultivating the habit of finishing your books will help turn you into a professional instead of an amateur. It will give you the discipline it takes to succeed.

Now we're going to talk about how to choose a great topic for your book. I just want you to realize that you're going to have dozens and maybe even hundreds of book ideas when we're done here. The key is to focus on just one idea and finish that one book first. "Get one done!" as T. Harv Eker says. Then you can get the second one, and the third one, and so on...

Picking Your Topic

The first step to deciding on your topic is to come up with as many book ideas as possible. You have to understand yourself and your potential before you can decide on the best course of action. *"Know thyself,"* as the old saying goes. *"This above all, to thine own self be true,"* said Shakespeare.

The truth is that your ever-expanding self-knowledge will be the greatest value you get from your writing. Even if you become a New York Times bestselling author, sell millions of books and become incredibly wealthy, the greatest value of all from writing is and always will be the self-knowledge that comes from the journey of becoming a great writer. Well, that's my opinion at least. The money is great too!

Here's the plan – I'm going to show you the 5 areas where you have the potential to write a bestselling book. Ready?

1. Passion

One of the ways to choose the topic of your book is to decide based on your passions. What do you love to learn? What do you love to do. What would you love to learn if money and time were no obstacle? What have you always dreamed of doing but haven't quite found the time for yet?

Often, our passions can be the greatest source of our inspiration and creative output.

2. Knowledge

What do you know a lot about already? What do your friends ask you for advice about? What do you love to teach to others, even without compensation or even being asked for advice? What do you already read about a lot? What do you know that most people don't know? What do you talk about at dinner parties?

Most of us tend to think that our knowledge isn't special. We think, "oh, everyone knows how cars work" but that's not true! I don't know how cars work. If someone could write a book that would quickly and easily explain to me the most important action steps I could take to properly maintain my car, I would gladly pay for it! Unfortunately, I haven't found one yet.

Your knowledge that you have so long discounted could be the source of an incredible career writing nonfiction books.

3. Expertise or Skill

What are you really frickin' good at? I mean, better at than anyone else you know? We all have our own unique skills. The problem with it is that we're often identified and made fun of because of our skills.

For example, I loved playing video games as a kid and teenager and so I was a "geek" or "dork" because of it. But I was really darn good at video games – better than all of my friends even. In fact, at one point around age 11, I was in the top 25 Starcraft players in the world according to the ranking ladder at the time. The problem with this is that if I told anyone that fact at a party, they would either laugh at me or just not care, unless they were all gamers.

The good news is, though, that millions of people all over the world love video games – and if I decided to write a book on video games, I would have a lot of loyal readers.

Do you see what's going on here? That little skill I have that is of absolutely no value in my social life or close relationships is incredibly valuable on the global marketplace. Had I known back then what I know now about publishing books, I would have been a bestselling author by age 12!

ACTION STEP

I'm guessing you have similar skills that you might even be embarrassed to talk about in social situations –

but you have those skills. And they could be huge assets for you when it comes to writing a book! What are your special, unique skills? Write them down and keep them in your journal.

4. Experience

What do you have experience in? Maybe you were in the military for several years and were trained in self-discipline, self-esteem and setting and achieving goals. Maybe you suffered horrible tragedies in your life and came through them even stronger. You could share your knowledge of how you overcame those struggles to inspire and instruct others now going through a hard time in life!

We all have incredibly valuable experiences in life that have instructed us and taught us important life lessons. You can share those lessons with others and make a huge difference in your readers' lives.

Market Research

Okay now you've got your list of potential book ideas. It's time to do some market research to understand the *likely* potential of each idea in terms of its monetary value. I say *likely* here and emphasize it because the truth is, there's no limit to your potential to write a bestselling book. You might research some obscure niche for a book like crocheting and become the runaway #1 bestseller in that category and sell millions of copies. The truth is ANYTHING is possible when it comes to writing and publishing books.

But we have NO WAY of knowing whether that's going to happen. So the best we can do is make an educated guess about how well your book *could* sell in a particular niche based on how books are *currently* selling in that niche. Make sense?

Step 1. Go To Amazon.com

Step 2. Search for Kindle books only

We're going to keep it to Kindle books because it's much easier to publish a Kindle book, it costs a whole lot less for first-time authors and it's also a lot easier to promote them using KDP Select and giveaways. These same principles I'm teaching you will work just fine for paperback or hardcover books, but I'm going to teach you the numbers based on Kindle books to make it easy for everyone to understand.

This link will take you to the Amazon search page only for the Kindle Store: *http://amzn.to/RLGyUr*

Step 3. Search Books In Your Niche

For example, for a dog training book, I would search "dog training books" and see what pops up. Then I would browse some of the top books that come up.

STEP 4. LOOK AT THE SALES RANK

You're looking for books that rank well in their category and have a lower sales rank. To give you an idea, a book that's ranked #1,000 in the Kindle Store sells about 100 copies a day. A book ranked #5,000 sells about 35 copies a day, and a book ranked #25,000 sells about 7 copies a day.

STEP 5. FIND THE TOP 5 BESTSELLING COMPARISONS

Now it's time to find the top 5 books in your niche. You can look at the books you find in the search, in the categories your book might be listed in and in the "Customers Who Bought This Item Also Bought" section. It's not crucial that you find the EXACT 5 top books in your category. Just do the best you can. You want to simply see what the competition is like and how well they are doing.

STEP 6. CALCULATE YOUR POTENTIAL

Now it's time to calculate the sales of your competitors' books. Always remember, the more the competition is selling, the better. That's because it means there's a bigger market for your book idea. Let's say you find the 5 top books in your niche are ranked #23,000, #26,000, #45,000, #77,000 and #100,000.

The first book two books are selling about 7 copies a day, the 3rd book is selling maybe 2 or 3 copies a day, and the last two are selling maybe 1 a day. Overall, that's only about 20 books a day being sold at best. I generally look for niches where at least 40 or 50 books a day are being sold. That way I know there's room for me to sell at least 10 books a day which would mean $500 to $1,000 a month in royalties, depending on my pricing.

Twenty sales a day is a pretty small number and I wouldn't recommend writing a book in that category from a profit standpoint unless you can 1) write a better book and 2) market your book better than the competition. Marketing is the key to success and the truth is that few authors today understand how to market effectively. But if you're just starting out with your first book, I would recommend writing in a niche where the top 5 books sell at least 50 copies a day combined. That way you will have a better chance of earning a decent income from your first book.

More Great Nonfiction Book Ideas

One of the best ways I've found personally to write a nonfiction book is to take something I love to do and then study it intensely and learn everything I can about it. Then I simply write the book using all my experience and knowledge as a new person who has just learned how to do it.

For example, when I first wrote The Kindle Publishing Bible, I had already been studying Kindle publishing and marketing for almost a year. I had published more than 10 books by then and felt I had attained enough expertise in the area to write a book on it. But at the same time, I was still "new" to the industry. I still had that new energy and excitement about the topic. That's really important!

Often, when we're true experts at something, we forget how to teach the basics and fundamentals of the subject to brand new people. Your nonfiction book could be the very first book your customer reads on your topic. If that's the case, you better communicate to them in a way that they can get it! Don't write over peoples' heads. It's easiest to do this if you're newer at something because you'll still have all those new questions fresh and your mind and you'll be able to help new people get all their questions answered.

So even if you've never skydived before, you could write a skydiving book for beginners within a year if you study it intensely and start skydiving yourself! This is a wonderful way to turn your passions, hobbies and interests into valuable and profitable nonfiction books.

Picking A Niche

Deciding on a specific niche for your book can be very helpful! For example, in the weight loss category your book on general weight loss might easily get lost in the crowd. However, a book on weight loss for moms after pregnancy would be a lot more likely to attract attention because it's so highly targeted.

If you were a mom who just had a new baby and wanted to lose weight, which book would you buy – "weight loss for everyone" or "weight loss for moms after pregnancy." It's a no-brainer!

One of my mentors, Ryan Lee, says "niche twice." He means, first pick your general category—like weight loss. Then, niche it down to a more focused group such as weight loss for women. Then, he says niche it down even one more time if you can, such as weight loss for moms who recently had a baby.

The benefit of having such a niche book is that your target market will buy your books instead of the competition's rather than having a generic book that doesn't really speak to anyone. This is especially important if you're a new author without a large blog, following or platform and you want to start breaking into the market with your books. If you already have a blog with 100,000 visitors, it's not nearly as important because you'll already be able to generate a lot of sales and exposure just using your established platform.

CHAPTER 4
CAPTURING IDEAS – THE KEY TO CREATIVITY

I've found that often I'll have a great idea and the next moment it's gone forever! The only way to keep those great ideas for new book titles or new book ideas for me is to record the ideas.

Most often, I do this in a journal or notebook I carry with me at all times. Whenever I leave the house, I have a notebook with me. I have one in the car. My fiancé keeps one in her purse for me. I have a notebook next to my computer and one next to my bed. I am always prepared to write down a good idea!

That might sound crazy or eccentric and maybe it is. But it works for me. Very, very well.

Have you ever sat down to write something and didn't know what to write? I used to feel that way all the time! But since I started recording all my ideas in a notebook, I can't even remember the last time that happened to me. It just doesn't happen anymore. I always have something to write. I can just browse at my notes and find an idea that inspires me and start writing without hesitation.

You see, I have this theory that each of us constantly is coming up with new ideas to improve our lives, write a bestselling book or just make progress in some area of life. But what do we do with those ideas? I used to just let them pass right on by like a pretty little cloud in the sky. And when they were gone, they were gone – poof! I couldn't remember them or do anything with them. But once I started recording my ideas, I realized how incredibly valuable they are.

I would urge you, if you're serious about being a successful writer, to write down ALL of your ideas in a notebook or journal. No matter how crazy, silly or stupid they sound, just write them down. This simple habit has changed my life in more ways than you could imagine.

Another great tool you can use is a tape recorder to record thoughts, ideas and passages for your book. I use an app on my iPhone called *QuickVoice* to record my thoughts or ideas when I'm in the car, traveling or don't have a notebook handy.

As a writer, you have to realize that your greatest assets are ideas. The more assets you have, the richer you will be (just ask any businessperson). If you want more money, capture more ideas.

22

Then once you capture them, it's time make your ideas become a reality through the right action.

CHAPTER 5
MASTERING THE WRITING PROCESS

Despite what the average author will tell you, there's more than one way to write a book. In fact, there are MILLIONS of ways to write a book and many of them don't even involve **you** writing!

For those of you who love to write and have no problem sitting on your laptop for a few hours a day to get it done, I'll share with you some of my proven strategies for getting even more writing work done at a higher quality.

But for those of you who hate to write, aren't good at it or would just prefer an easier way, I'm going to show you some incredible strategies to get **other people** to write your book for you. And you can get someone to write your book for you for less than $1,000 by the way – you don't have to pay a lot of money to have someone else create your great book with you.

How To Master The Writing Process

The writing process is a mystery to most people. Even some of the most successful writers I've met have no idea how they do what they do! If you ask them for advice on how to become a better writer, they'll give you vague answers like "just write more" or "find something that inspires you to write." And while both of those answers are indeed true and very powerful for those who understand and use them, it's far too vague for you and I to get the best results we possibly can.

And that's what I want for you – I want you to get the best writing results you possibly can. That means you write more, you write faster and you write higher quality material.

I'm going to share with you my writing process now. Feel free to use what works best for you and discard whatever doesn't work. I'm not going to try to tell you that MY way is the BEST way – that's nonsense! My way works great for me. It might not work great for you. But I guarantee you you'll learn a heck of a lot from how I write.

The following is my 5-step writing process for success. However, I don't ALWAYS follow these 5 steps in order and I don't always follow 1 step at a time. I've found it's much more enjoyable and productive to allow myself to be flexible with my writing. Furthermore, I've never consciously *decided* to do this 5-step writing process until I had to write this book. I've been using this 5-

step process for years completely unconsciously and so I never stop in the middle of writing and tell myself "okay Tom, now it's time to go to step 4!" Instead, I just allow myself to write and always strive to make forward progress. I urge you to do the same.

STEP 1. PRE-WRITING

For me, pre-writing is a huge key to my success. The truth is that I don't always pre-write – sometimes I get an instant flash of inspiration and just start writing. But that doesn't happen very often. What happens most of the time is that I pre-write my book and then I move into the real writing.

What is pre-writing? It's basically pre-formatting your book to prepare it and you for success.

For example, now when I come up with a new book idea, I will take one of my older book templates and create a new book document with a new name. Then, I'll go to the title page and change the title of the book to a new "title placeholder." I don't even need to know the title of the book yet, I just need to know what it's about.

For example, for this book my title placeholder is *How to write more nonfiction books* – a horrible title, I know. But it's not meant to be final. It's meant to take the place of my title for now and help me create the image of my book fully formed so that I can start filling it in.

Next, I will go to the back of my book and edit my About The Author section, Other Books By Tom Corson-Knowles, the Review Request, and any bonus material I might offer. For example, I've created a list of my personal favorite motivational videos and I include that list in most of my books.

Altogether, when I'm done pre-writing, I'll often have 500 to 3,000 words in my book already done! That's before I've even started writing! I don't know about you but that makes me feel pretty darn good when I look at the Microsoft Word count at the bottom of the page and see that I've already got a couple hundred or even a thousand words or more done and I haven't even started to write yet!

I initially learned a trick similar to this many years ago from a source I have long since forgotten. Basically, someone had told me to format my books in Microsoft Word to make it look like a book, complete with page numbers and what not. Well, I tried that and it was nice but it didn't do the trick for me. Pre-writing does the trick for me. Regardless, I encourage you to find something you can do to create a new book document that makes it **come alive** even before you start writing. It will help give you that extra motivation to start writing and keep writing once your book starts to actually look like a book instead of a 100% empty document that you have to magically fill up.

It's just a strange little fact of human nature that it's a lot easier to go from 500 to 50,000 words than it is to go from 0 to 500. My advice: get the 500 words down first and then start writing!

Step 2. Planning

Planning is where you outline the basic ideas and points of your book. You can just write out the words to create a "book skeleton" if you will. Some people spend a lot of time planning their books. They'll even write out all the chapter titles on index cards and have sections on each index card for major points or subheadings in each chapter. That's all fine and dandy, but for me simpler is better (and a whole lot faster).

For example, for this book I started with this skeleton:

Topic (passion, knowledge, expertise, experience, market research)

Writing (ghostwriting, interviews, how to write better, etc)

That was it! It took me less than 2 minutes to create that initial plan and it inspired me enough to start Step 3 – creative writing.

Step 3. Creative Writing

I call the first part of writing *creative writing* because it's all about using your creativity. It's not about editing. It's not about research. It's not about facts or figures or charts or pictures or graphics or references or footnotes. It's just about writing your ideas and thoughts on paper and letting it flow unrestricted with no distractions!

Most new writers try to do too much when they start writing. They get this great idea, write 200 words and then "Oh shoot, I can't remember if there are 30 or 31 days in November!" And so you minimize your writing document, open up your web browser and start Googling. The problem with this is that it will DESTROY your writing output and productivity (by the way, there are only 30 days in November).

It's like telling a young child to draw a picture and then every 5 minutes you offer them a cookie. You're not going to get that picture done anytime soon and it's probably going to look like crap with all those crumbs all over it.

Instead, when you start writing, just write! Don't research. Don't close your writing document. Don't talk to anyone. Don't try to edit while you type. Don't worry about spelling. Don't look at a dictionary. Don't do anything that distracts you from writing the ideas flowing through your mind.

If you follow these simple rules, you'll find your writing productivity will increase dramatically. For me, my writing productivity increased 500% by following these little rules. Imagine if you could write 5 books in the time you had previously been writing only one. Do you think that would make a difference in your results? Of course it would!

TIPS TO STAY IN CREATIVE WRITING

Instead of searching for hyperlinks online to refer readers to the correct website just write (link) and skip a line. Then, when you come back to edit the book, you can remember to insert the correct link.

Likewise, instead of researching a particular statistic or idea online, just write XXX and skip a line. For example, in one of my business books I was writing about the business failure rate in America. I couldn't remember how many businesses failed in the first 5 years (it's 55% according to *Illusions of Entrepreneurship*, while other sources say as high as 80%). But instead of looking up those facts and screwing up your creative writing process, just write XXX, skip a line and do your research during the editing phase.

Step 4. Editing

Now it's time to edit your writing. Once you're "done" with creative writing, or as done as you feel you need to be at this time, you can go back over your work and start editing. This is where you'll fix any typos or sentence fragments. You'll research any facts or figures you forgot about and insert any hyperlinks that you had intended to include. You'll also want to insert pictures, graphs or any other media type that you'd like to include in the book.

Personally, when I go through my first edit, I always find that I also need to write more. Maybe a section is too brief or unclear for readers, so I need to elaborate on a point or even add ideas and resources that I hadn't even thought about the first time around.

At this point, some of my books may be perfectly organized while others may not necessarily be organized into chapters yet. If you need to create new chapters, break up text, move passages around or even delete sections of your book, now is the time to do it.

Again, even though I'm now in the editing phase of the book, I'm often still coming up with new ideas for adding more value, insights and knowledge into the book. The key, however, is to know when enough is enough. For example, I could continue this book to talk about how to market your books, how to do advance competitive research, book analytics, cover design, title selection, the psychology of writing, how to treat your writing like a business, and dozens of other topics that, although are all related to writing books, aren't really what this book is all about. And if I put all that information into this one book, it would be over 500 pages! And no one would read it or buy it because it would be so bulky and complete information overload.

Keep your books simple, sweet, short and to the point. You'll notice I don't have a lot of stories in my books. Sure, I've got one or two good stories that are on point, if that. But not much more. I don't want to bore my readers with facts about my mother-in-law or stories about some trip to Europe that no one gives a crap about but me. I just want to help my readers solve their problem.

Many nonfiction writers are insecure about their ability to do this. That's why they'll write a 350 page book what could be done just as well at 50 pages and saved the reader a heck of a lot of time. My time is valuable. Therefore, I assume my reader's time is valuable. I don't waste it with fluff, irrelevant stories or drivel.

Step 4.5 Crowdsourcing

Crowdsourcing is a great way to have other people help you improve your book. Most authors will give their book manuscript to their wife or family or friends or even a fellow author and have them review it for typos, grammatical errors, fact-checking and other recommendations. That's a wonderful way to get free advice and help on improving your book.

It's not the same as hiring a professional editor (unless you happen to know a professional editor who's willing to help you out for free) but it's still good enough, most of the time. You can also ask your friends and followers on social media to read the book and give you feedback.

This step isn't necessary but it can be very helpful for some projects. Personally, I rarely do this anymore because 1) I write too many books and my family and friends got tired of reading them and 2) I'm now more confident in my writing skills. It doesn't mean I don't make mistakes (I certainly make plenty!). It just means I don't care if my book has a typo or a link is broken. Sure, I do my VERY BEST to make sure that doesn't happen but, at the end of the day, one typo isn't going to ruin my book. And 99% of the time, I'll have a reader or friend email me once the book is published and let me know about the typos or errors – then I just fix them immediately and re-upload the corrected version of the book. Voila!

Step 5. Formatting

Now that you've edited your book, it's time to format! If you're writing for Kindle, it's pretty simple and straightforward and you can learn how to do it yourself in about an hour step by step in *The Kindle Formatting Bible*.

If you're writing a paperback, formatting is going to be a lot more difficult and I would recommend hiring a professional. Either way, your formatting needs to get done and it needs to be done right. Nothing will piss off readers more than a book that's hard to read due to atrocious formatting.

The good news is that if you're publishing on Kindle, you can upload your book and then test the formatting. If you need to make any changes or fixes, you can do so, re-upload your book and have the new perfectly formatted book live within 24 hours most of the time.

For paperback or hardcover books, you don't have that luxury which is why I highly recommend hiring a professional.

What About Re-Editing?

The truth is, just one edit is often not enough to get your book how you want it. You might want to edit your book once, set it aside for a day and then edit it again 24 hours later to keep yourself from dying of editing-itis, a tragic condition known to kill some writer's careers.

I would encourage you to edit your book as much as it needs to be done but not too much.

You'll know when it's too much if:

- You spend more than 4 weeks editing
- You edit more than 10 times
- You can't remember how many times you edited it already
- You find yourself re-writing the same section over and over 10 times even though there are no typos, grammatical errors or really anything wrong with it at all.

If you notice yourself editing too much, it's time to publish your frickin' book and move on! The good news is that you can ALWAYS come out with a 2nd edition. The bad news is that perfectionism is a disease and you better kill it before it kills your career.

CHAPTER 6
HOW TO WRITE WITHOUT WRITING

This is my favorite part! Not because I use these strategies every single day (I still love writing and would never give it up), but because when I teach this to new would-be authors, their eyes light up and their mouth starts to drool at the possibilities. I love teaching which is why I write nonfiction.

Even if you're an avid writer like me and never want to give it up, you'll still get a TON of value out of this chapter so I highly recommend you read it.

The following are strategies you can use to have someone else write your book for you, or simply to speed up your own writing. All of these strategies can be mixed and matched and used together for even better results.

Interview Others

Interviewing is a great way to get new information, ideas and bonus content for your books. For example, for my book *The Kindle Publishing Bible*, I interviewed several bestselling authors who all earn several thousand dollars a month or more selling Kindle books. I then just gave away those interviews for free as a *surprise bonus* to readers. This was a win-win-win all around. It was great for me because I learned a few new marketing tidbits myself and it dramatically increased the value of my book. It was a win for the authors I interviewed because they got tons of free exposure. And it was a win for readers because they got to learn a lot more about kindle publishing and marketing and they could do it in video format, not just by reading my book. You too can access those videos at the back of this book.

In the case above, I interviewed those authors just as a bonus. I didn't add their ideas to my book – but you could! You could interview 5 or 10 top experts in your field and incorporate some of their ideas in your book. Now, I'm not telling you to do this unethically or steal their ideas. Of course, you would have to tell them ahead of time what the purpose of the interview was and you should always give them credit for their ideas.

Another great idea is to interview potential readers. Ask them about their problems, challenges, struggles and ideas. What kind of help do they need in your area of expertise? What questions do they have about the topic? You can then compile those questions into a very helpful FAQ or you can just make sure to answer each of them in the book itself. That research is golden and it will also often produced guaranteed buyers of your book before it's even written! I've interviewed potential readers before for books and had dozens of people tell me they would buy my book the day it came out – and they did! That's not just smart writing, it's smart marketing.

WHERE TO FIND EXPERTS TO INTERVIEW

One of the easiest ways to find experts to interview is to use the free service HARO *helpareporter.com*. You can post a query as a media person looking to interview experts for your book on your topic. Make sure to be very specific about what kind of experts you want to interview, what the topic will be, how long the interview will be and how soon you need to schedule it to avoid dozens of responses from unqualified sources.

With just one post on HARO, I've gotten as many as 127 responses from experts looking to be interviewed! So if you're looking to interview some of the top people in your industry, HARO is a great way to connect with them and it doesn't cost a dime.

Have Someone Interview You

Another great way to get content for your book is to simply have someone interview you. Most of us talk A LOT faster than we write. And talking also accesses a different part of our brains, meaning we can access different ideas, memories and resources when we talk. So if you don't like to write or if you're having trouble writing, or even if you just want to try a new way of writing, have someone interview you about your ideas.

You could have your partner, family member, friend, associate, colleague or even a complete stranger interview you – it doesn't really matter. Just find someone who can do a good job of asking the right questions to draw out the ideas from you. Then, you can record the interview on video camera or just with an audio recorder.

When you're done with the interview, you can have someone transcribe it and turn it into a book. Or you can simply listen to it again and write the ideas that you shared in the interview. Or, you can just give the tapes to a ghostwriter and have them write the entire book for you! There are many ways you can use this information to create your book.

Hire a Ghostwriter

Hiring a ghostwriter is a wonderful way to get your book written if you need someone to help with research or if you just want to outsource the whole writing books thing. I've used ghostwriters many times with great success. However, before you go out and hire the first person you meet, make sure you know what you're doing!

People have many different ideas about what ghostwriting means and prices range from $100 for 10,000 words all the way to $250,000 for a complete book.

I don't use ghostwriters to write the whole book for me. Instead, I use a ghostwriter to do a lot of the basic research and outlining for the book and fill it in with good content for my readers. The ghostwriter is basically doing my creative writing for me in this case and then I make sure to go back and edit the book thoroughly as well as adding in more content, usually an introduction and conclusion and any other information I'd like to add. I usually use a ghostwriter when I'm writing about a topic that I am passionate about but am not a complete expert in (for example, gardening). I know a lot about gardening with vertical aeroponic gardens through personal experience and interviewing experts, but when it comes to what kinds of fertilizers to use or how to get rid of certain pests, I have my ghostwriter do that research for me.

In that case, I just post my request on the **_Craigslist San Francisco Writing Gigs_** section because it's free to post there and thousands of writers will see it. I often get 5 to 10 responses each time I post and if I'm not happy with the candidates, I'll simply repost it until I find the right person for me. I generally pay between $150 and $300 for 10,000 words. I wouldn't recommend paying much more for a ghostwriter if you plan to do a lot of editing and re-writing of the book because it's not worth it. If you want a complete book written for you, you're going to have to pay a lot more and the quality probably won't be nearly what you expected anyway unless you're paying $50,000 or more for a very, very experienced ghostwriter.

WORK FOR HIRE CONTRACT

Make sure you have a 'Work For Hire' contract or at least a written agreement! I'm no attorney and I can't give you legal advice so you'll have to find your own attorney to consult you on this, but I would highly recommend getting a signed contract before you ever hire a ghostwriter.

Contracts can help protect you in case of a lawsuit, but in most cases contracts will be much more helpful by simply getting everything in writing and making sure you both agree to what needs to be done, who needs to do it, when it needs to be done by and how much it will all cost. If you are willing to spend a few extra hours of work upfront to make sure that you have very clear communication and expectations of each other, your partnerships will work out a lot better. You'll probably end up saving a lot of time and stress as well in the long-run over disagreements that could have been avoided.

At the end of the day, it's up to you to decide how to approach these legal issues with proper legal advice (ie, not my advice).

Audio Recording

Audio recording is another great tool to use when writing a book. I use an app on my iPhone called QuickVoice. And it's amazing! I just press a button and it records whatever I say. Then I can email myself the files or put them into Dropbox and listen to them while I write.

I often find myself coming up with great ideas for book titles, or a new section of a book, or a new marketing idea and I'll use my voice recorder app to record that information so I can use it to my advantage.

I recommend you do the same! Don't let a great idea come and go unrecorded. If you do, you're just shooting yourself in the foot.

Chapter 7
Overcoming The 7 Deadly Writing Obstacles

1. Fear

Fear is the #1 killer of success as a writer. It's why most people wake up every morning and work in a 9-5 job they hate. It's why more heart attacks happen on Monday mornings while people are on their way to an unfulfilling job. It's why writers will throw away their manuscript instead of self-publishing or dealing with the rejection of pursuing a publishing contract. It's why we put off making the important decisions in our life. It's why we're more concerned with what other people think of us than we are with what we think of ourselves.

We're afraid of what others will think and say about us. We're afraid of failing. We're afraid of succeeding. We're afraid of getting rejected. We're afraid of getting published and not selling, or having readers hate our work. We're afraid of 1-star and 2-star reviews.

Well guess what! Harry Potter Book 1 has 94 1-star reviews and 88 2-star reviews and I don't even have those many negative reviews on my 20+ books combined! And guess what else? J.K. Rowling sells way more books than I do.

Fear is just an illusion. It says that you shouldn't finish your book because others might not like it. The truth is if your book becomes successful, changes the world and helps millions of people live a happier life, millions of others probably won't like it! Some will hate it and some will love it. That's just how the world works. If you just try to please everyone, you end up pleasing no one.

A parable in the bible says Jesus gave a great speech one day to thousands and thousands of people. At the end of his incredible presentation, there were some believers, some mockers, and some who just didn't understand.

If Jesus couldn't get 100% positive response then why would you ever expect your book to get a 100% positive response? That's just not how the world works.

Successful writers understand that fear is an illusion and they act in spite of fear. Are you willing to take action even in the face of your fear?

2. Procrastination

Procrastination will murder your success and rob you blind if you let it! You have to have the self-control, self-motivation and self-discipline to keep making progress with your writing. Procrastination is simply a habit and we all suffer from it to some extent.

The reason we procrastinate is because we associate more pain with taking action than we do with not taking action. For example, if you're procrastinating on publishing your book, it's probably because you associate pain with the unknown aspects of publishing, potential rejections and other challenges. That pain you anticipate is stronger than the anticipated pleasure of publishing your book. That's why you don't do it!

If you want to do a quick exercise to get rid of your procrastination instantly, just grab a piece of paper and a pen right now. Write down at the top of the blank page of paper what action you're procrastinating and putting off. For example, "publishing my book." Then, on the right side write "pain" and the left side "pleasure" with a dividing line down the middle. In the pain side, write down all the reasons why taking action could be painful, such as "I'd rather watch TV" or "I don't want to be rejected" or "what if it doesn't sell?" – but the catch is you have to write in the tiniest possible handwriting you can. Write the painful outcomes as small as humanly possible – if you can't read it then you're doing it right.

47

Now, on the side under pleasure, write down all the reasons why taking that action will bring you pleasure such as "I could become a best-selling author" or "I could earn a great income from my royalties" or "I would gain the respect of my peers and readers." Write the pleasurable outcomes in your normal handwriting or maybe even a bit bigger than normal – you want it to take up the whole pleasure side of the page.

When you're done writing the pain and pleasure outcomes, look at the paper. You should clearly now see that you're going to get a lot more pleasure from getting it done than by putting it off. Now you have *reframed your perspective* and you should be excited now to go get it done rather than anxious about it.

3. Indecision

Indecision will also murder your success and rob you blind! Indecision comes from insecurity in ourselves as well as old habits. Indecision is really just another form of procrastination – but instead of hesitating to take action, we're hesitating to decide something. You might be indecisive about what the title of your book should be or whether to self-publish or find an agent.

General Colin Powell said, *"Indecision has cost the American government, American businesses, and the American people billions of dollars more than the wrong decision."* And he's right!

Fundamentally, we are indecisive because we have low self-esteem. Maybe we're repeating negative thoughts in our head or we were unconsciously taught as a child not to be decisive. Maybe we got punished in the past for making a decision that someone else didn't like. Whatever it is doesn't really matter. The key is to understand that you can ALWAYS change your decisions later. You can publish your book today on Kindle and then two days from now, change the title. It's okay to make changes! But the good news is, when you start being decisive and making decisions quickly, you'll find you don't need to change your decisions very often. Most of the time, you'll do it just right and you will have saved yourself a lot of time, worry and energy by making a good decision without procrastinating. And when you do have to make a tough decision to change something important, you'll get it done right away so you can move on with your life.

Are there any important decisions you've been putting off? Write them down write now in your notebook and commit to making a decision before your head hits the pillow tonight.

4. Perfectionism

Perfectionism is highly related to procrastination and indecision as well. Oftentimes, it's our perfectionism that keeps us from finishing a project or publishing a book. "It's not quite ready yet..." we keep telling ourselves. But the truth is it will NEVER be ready according to your perfect standards! THERE IS NO PERFECT BOOK AND THERE NEVER WILL BE.

If you're trying to write a perfect book, you'll die before you ever reach that goal. Look at all the New York Times bestsellers. I've read many professionally published books that had typos, grammatical errors or phrases or sentences that didn't make sense or were even just factually incorrect. Despite having a whole publishing house and a team of editors, those New York Times bestsellers still aren't perfect! So how could little old you possibly write a perfect book? You can't! So don't even try.

Here's what you can do: write the best book you're capable of writing today. Then publish it. If you want to make changes or edits to it later, that's totally fine. You can come out with a 2nd or 3rd or 797th edition. You don't have to be perfect to become a bestselling author – but you do have to finish writing and editing and publish your book.

5. Lack of Money

A lot of would-be authors say they don't have enough cash to write and publish a book. Nonsense! It's cheaper today to publish a book than it ever has been in the history of the world.

I've published books on Amazon Kindle for as little as $5 – that's right, just five dollars! If you learn how to write the book yourself, edit it yourself, format it yourself, publish it yourself, and hire a cover designer on Fiverr.com for $5, then you have a $5 book. Heck, if you use the GIMP graphic design software and know some graphic design skills, you could even create your own book cover and publish a book at no cost other than your time.

Now I'm not telling you to go the ultra-cheap route, but if money is an issue then why not? Don't let money stop you from writing and publishing a book. There's no excuse for that anymore!

6. Lack of Knowledge

Knowledge can be a huge stumbling block for new authors. I know it was knowledge combined with fear that stopped me from publishing my first book over 6 years ago! It took me 6 years to publish my first book because I didn't know how to.

You don't have that excuse anymore! You can learn how to format and upload your book to Kindle in less than an hour with *The Kindle Formatting Bible*.

7. Lack of Vision

Lack of vision can be just as deadly to your success. It means you can't see where you're going. You have no goals or dreams you're shooting for. You can't see how it's going to happen. You can't even imagine writing a book – where would you start?

Jack Canfield tells a wonderful story that illustrates this concept. Imagine you were driving from California to New York at night in your car. Your headlights on your car only show about the next 200 feet of road. You can't possibly see what's beyond the next 200 feet. But you can still drive from California to New York at night without a problem. Why? Because you have a road map or GPS. You have directions. And, even more importantly, you just know in your mind that you're going to get there if you keep moving forward.

If you can see your goals and dreams in your mind as clearly as you can see that driving your car will get you from point A to point B, you'll have no problem becoming successful. With a great vision, when challenges or obstacles come up, you just go over, under, around or through them. You do whatever it takes to succeed because you know deep down in your heart that you have what it takes.

Do you have a strong vision for your life and your writing career?

CHAPTER 8
WRITING TIPS AND TRICKS

You want to write faster? You want to produce more, better work? Then sit your ass down and write!

You can't cheat success! You have to invest the time. You have to write. Sitting down in your chair isn't writing. Looking at your computer isn't writing. Surfing the internet isn't writing. Talking to all your writer friends isn't writing. Writing is writing.

The only thing that counts is your action. Anyone can come up with a great idea for "the next Harry Potter." Can you write it though? That's the test of greatness. It's not even about the idea – it's about being willing to do the work required to turn your ideas into a reality.

Finish Writing Mid-Sentence

I learned this tip from Tim Ferriss who recommends always to stop writing at the end of the day mid-sentence. That way, when you sit back down to write, all you have to do is finish that sentence and you're off and running.

I've found this simple practice dramatically improves my writing output because I no longer spend several minutes every time I sit down to write thinking about what to write next – I already know all I have to do is finish that sentence!

Write It Now!

If I find myself in the middle of reading a book or making lunch and all of a sudden start thinking about what to write next in my book, I just go sit down and write it. As soon as the inspiration hits me, I'll go to my computer if I can and write it down. Then, when the thought or passage is finished, I just get back up and continue what I was doing. This is just like the recording ideas habit we talked about before except I'm actually implementing the ideas right away instead of capturing them for later.

Diversions

Diversions are not interruptions – they are intentional things you do to interrupt your writing when it's not going well or to give your mind and body a break so that you can write even better.

For example, if I find myself struggling to write anything or if I get stuck in a certain passage or section of my book, I'll give myself a diversion. For example, I might get up and go for a walk. I might go swimming or play some music and jam out for a few minutes. I just do something to *change my state* as they say in NLP. As soon as I'm done with the diversion, I go back to writing. If I find myself needing more than one or two diversions, I'll either quit for the day or just force myself to continue writing.

This keeps me from developing bad writing habits such as sitting at the computer but not actually writing or avoiding writing altogether by taking too many diversions.

Exercise

Exercise is crucial for keeping up your writing output. Many writers can get posture problems and aches and pains from sitting at the computer all day. It's a good idea to stand up and walk around, do some jumping jacks or pushups or other exercise to get your blood moving and then get back to writing. I try to take exercise breaks as often as I think of them.

Some people recommend setting an alarm every 30 or 60 minutes to get up and move around which is a good idea if you need the reminder. Personally, I find I work better without any distractions like that but do what works best for you. Don't just sit for 2, 4, 6 or 8 hours straight! Make sure to get up and move around.

Interruptions

Interruptions from your family, friends, phone calls or surfing the web can kill your writing productivity. Try to write in an office or room where you're all alone and it's quiet and peaceful. Tell your family not to disturb you unless it's an emergency. Turn your phone on silent unless you're expecting an urgent call. Close your web browsers and just focus on writing!

Take a Walk

I often find that some of my best ideas come from my time walking or running. It's a great way to get your mind off all the worries and drama of your life and just clear your head. It's very meditative and can help you come up with new ideas that you can implement when you come home from your walk.

If you meditate, your meditation practice can also be hugely beneficial to your writing.

Music

Music can help dramatically improve your writing output as well as your enjoyment of the writing process. Sometimes I love to listen to music while I write and others times I find it distracting and enjoy the silence. Just experiment and see what works best for you.

I would highly recommend trying to listen to baroque music or classical music while you work. Some people say it helps improve learning and creativity. I grew up listening to Alternative, Rock, Hip Hop and Rap and hated classical music. But when I started listening to baroque music while working, I noticed it did help improve my writing output quite a bit. You'll never know unless you try it!

Backup Your Books

Nothing is worse than losing a book! If your computer crashes, gets a virus, or something else happens, you better make sure your books are backed up! There are lots of backup programs you can get for your computer that will automatically backup your files for you like **Crashplan** but it does cost about $60 a year.

You can also use free software like **Dropbox** and **Google Drive** to backup your books for you.

Generating Ideas

One of the easiest ways to generate new ideas for books is to become an expert and answer questions. You can sign up for free at **AllExperts.com** and **quora.com** answer questions for people on your area of expertise. Then, you can take the most frequently asked questions and make sure to include those answers and information in your books on the topic. It's also a great way to get free exposure for your name and your work!

BONUS INTERVIEWS

I told you earlier about the interviews I did for The Kindle Publishing Bible. I hunted down some of the top Kindle authors on the planet and I'll be interviewing them over the coming weeks. All of these authors earn several thousand dollars a month in royalties from Kindle books and some earn far more.

But they won't be pitching you on their newest book, not even close. They will only be sharing their most precious marketing techniques, inspirational stories and ideas for new and budding authors like you who want to earn a full-time income as an author.

The first interview with Bev Flaxington, two-time bestselling and Gold-award winning author is now live and you can watch it for free here on YouTube:

http://bit.ly/SrDcos

The second interview with Oli Hille, international bestselling author is live now as well. Watch it here on YouTube:

http://bit.ly/ZtJFWN

THE KINDLE BIBLE SERIES

If you liked this book then you will love the rest of the books in the Kindle Bible Series.

The Kindle Formatting Bible is the next step in the process. It takes you through step-by-step formatting tutorials to show you how to format your book for Kindle using Microsoft Word. It also walks you through the process of uploading your book to Kindle.

The Kindle Publishing Bible is the next book in the series. It's all about the marketing! The book shows you how to choose bestselling book titles and provides a step-by-step marketing system that anyone can use to sell a lot more books quickly.

Kindle Success Stories is a recent addition to the series. In this book, I researched the top self-published Kindle authors in the world and asked them to share their stories, lessons and tips for new and aspiring authors. Many of these authors have sold hundreds of thousands of Kindle eBooks, and some of them have sold millions.

SPECIAL FACEBOOK GROUP

Come join our Facebook group just for authors like you who want to network, share ideas, collaborate and connect with other like-minded authors. In this group we'll be sharing our successes, marketing tips and strategies with each other so that we can all continue to succeed as authors.

Come join us here on Facebook:

www.facebook.com/groups/KindlePublishers

FREE BLOGGING FOR BUSINESS TRAINING

If you're a business owner and want to learn how to start a blog for your business that makes a profit, I've developed a free online training program to teach you everything from how to build your blog to getting traffic to monetizing it.

You can get the free training at:

BlogBusinessSchool.com

THE COMPLETE
KINDLE PUBLISHING COURSE

Want to learn more about Kindle publishing and marketing?

As a way of saying "thank you" for downloading and reading this book, I want to give you a special discount on my premier Kindle publishing and marketing course. With over 40 videos and 7+ hours of training, it's the most comprehensive course in the world on Kindle publishing and marketing.

You can get access to it here:

www.udemy.com/kindle-publishing-course

Make sure to redeem your coupon code for 10% off:

SpecialReaderDiscount1

WANT TO GET PUBLISHED?

If you've written one or several books and just want to focus on your writing, you might want to consider publishing with TCK Publishing founded by Tom Corson-Knowles. We'll help you choose the right title and help with market research ahead of time so your book will sell better. We also do all the formatting for Kindle, cover design, publishing and a lot of marketing for our clients.

Many of our clients have already become bestselling authors. Will you be next?

We publish both nonfiction and fiction books. Learn more at:

www.tckpublishing.com/publishing

CONNECT WITH TOM

Thank you so much for taking the time to read this book. I'm excited for you to start your path to creating the life of your dreams as a Kindle author.

If you have any questions of any kind, feel free to contact me directly at: ***Tom@TCKPublishing.com***

You can follow me on Twitter: ***@JuiceTom***

And connect with me on Facebook:

www.facebook.com/tomcorsonknowles

You can check out my publishing blog for the latest updates here:

www.TCKpublishing.com

I'm wishing you the best of health, happiness and success!

Here's to you!

Tom Corson-Knowles

ABOUT THE AUTHOR

TOM CORSON-KNOWLES is the #1 Amazon best-selling author of *The Kindle Publishing Bible* and *How To Make Money With Twitter*, among others. He lives in Kapaa, Hawaii. Tom loves educating and inspiring other entrepreneurs to succeed and live their dreams.

Learn more at:

www.Amazon.com/author/business

OTHER BOOKS BY
TOM CORSON-KNOWLES

Secrets of the Six-Figure Author: Mastering the Inner Game of Writing, Publishing and Marketing Books

Systemize, Automate, Delegate: How to Grow a Business While Traveling, on Vacation and Taking Time Off

Ninja Book Marketing Strategies

The Kindle Publishing Bible: How To Sell More Kindle eBooks On Amazon

The Kindle Formatting Bible: How To Format Your eBook For Kindle Using Microsoft Word

Kindle Success Stories: How Average People Like You Are Earning a Fortune Self-Publishing Kindle Ebooks

How To Make Money With Twitter

The Blog Business Book: How To Start A Blog And Turn It Into A Six Figure Online Business

101 Ways To Start A Business For Less Than $1,000

Facebook For Business Owners: Facebook Marketing For Fan Page Owners and Small Businesses

Rich by 22: How To Achieve Business Success at an Early Age

How To Reduce Your Debt Overnight: A Simple System To Eliminate Credit Card And Consumer Debt

The Network Marketing Manual: Work From Home And Get Rich In Direct Sales

Dr. Corson's Top 5 Nutrition Tips

The Vertical Gardening Guidebook: How To Create Beautiful Vertical Gardens, Container Gardens and Aeroponic Vertical Tower Gardens at Home

See a full list of Tom's published books at:

www.Amazon.com/Author/Business

Made in the USA
San Bernardino, CA
20 July 2014